THE PROCTOR FAMILY HISTORY

England to Tennessee

By

Katherine Fletcher

ORIGINS OF THE PROCTOR FAMILY

One of the early records of the Proctor family in England is found in Downton Parish,Wiltshire. The town of Salisbury was the county seat of Wiltshire. The Proctor family there were a family of such influence and importance as to have been represented in Parliment in 1747 by the Honorable George Proctor. (from The Founders of the Mass Bay Colony)

Northumberland and London, England

This family was first found in Cambridgeshire where they held a family seat from ancient times. Some of the first settlers were Thomas Procter who went to Newfoundland in 1725, Mark Procter and James Procter who went to St. Johns Newfoundland. John Procter settled in Virginia in 1607.

The ENGLISH MOTTO for the Proctor family is "Always Faithful"

The crest states that they came to England with William the Conqueror (1066) from France.

The name "proctor" comes from the latin Procurator. which meant an official who was appointed to take care of something involving human affairs. The important part of the word is "cura". which is care, and this is the part that has been dropped. In the middle ages when the church was not only a spiratual support and a santuary, but also a political force to be delt with, a large part of the judicial function of the government was carried on in the Ecclesiastical Courts. This required the services of ecclesastical lawyer who came to be called Procurators. Following is a list of some of the earliest known appearences of the name Procurator or Proctor, with the year and the documents where they were found.

Thomas le Procuratour, --County of Lincolnshire Hundred Rolls, 1273

John le Procuratour of Lincolnshire.

William le Procuratour,--Northumberland Assize Rolls 1279

Johanna la Proketour. Yorkshire Subsidy Rolls.

John Proketour,--Durham, Feodarum Prioratus Dunelmensis, 1326

Williamus Proktour,--West Riding, Yorkshire Poll Tax 1379

 It was not until this time that surnames became commonly used. In the case of Proctor, like Carpenter, Miller, Fisher, etc. it was used first mearlu as an identification through one's occupation, and later as a surname in the modern sense when the "le" or "la" was dropped. The influence of the French language was still strongly apparent as a result of the Norman Conquest over two hundred years earlier.

SUMMARY OF THIS LINE

This line goes from England (1390) to Salem, Massachusetts, Virginia, North Carolina and on to West Tennessee. Some of these Proctors from England were the settlers of Jamestown and went through Bacon's Rebellion and the Indian massacres. . Some of the connecting lines are found in Kentucky and Arkansas.

Some disturbing stories about not so nice George Proctor and the accusations he beat two servants to death.   He was also very abusive to his wife.   Also the sad story of John and his wife Elizabeth who migrated to Salem MA and were accused of being witches during the Salem Witch Trials. John was killed by hanging.   There is a connection to Pochantas through her husband John Rolfe who sailed with John Graye Proctor from England.   There are many interesting stories and wills from this line of Proctor's. The line goes deep back to England.

GENERATION ONE

Katie Proctor (1919-1992) and Joseph Woodrow Forbes (1912-1988)

Katie was born in Munford, TN and died in Memphis, TN. They married on October 24, 1936 in Arkansas.

Joseph was born and died in Millington, TN.   His parents are Joseph Edward Forbes and Bertha Delilah Davidson.

GENERATION TWO

Ernest Blaydes Proctor (1886-1970) and Willie Florence Jones (1892-1973)

Ernest was born and died in Munford, TN.   Willie Jones also born and died in Memphis, TN,.

Ernest was in World War I.   They married in 1908.

Their children:

Charmanise Trilby Proctor – married Gilbert Martin in 1936

Ernest Blaydes

Eureka James (1915-

Katie Proctor (1919-1992) – married Joseph Woodrow Forbes

Headrick Darrell Proctor (1928) – married Betty Jane Pickard

GENERATION THREE

Robert Meredith Proctor (1850-1922) and Catherine
Breckenridge Freedle (Kate Proctor) (1860-1932)

Robert was born in Orange County, North Carolina. According
to his death certificate below he died of senility and nephritis.
He was a farmer

 Catherine born and died in Tipton, TN. Her parents are
Alexander W. Freedle and Emilie Adeline McGuire. Her
grandparents are A. Willis Freedle (1796-1882) and Elizabeth
Betsy Yarbrough (1791-1872)

Their children:

Minnie H. (1880)

Wilks Booth (1883-1933) born in Tipton, TN / died in Phoenix, Arizona / married Lucy Viola ?.   He died of Tuberculosis.

Olivy (1885)

Earnest (1886)

Jessie J. (1888)

Robert Alexander (1890-1971) married Nancy Denell Edmonds

Donald A. (1893-1924) died at age 33 from Tuberculosis

Charles Hedick (1897-1919) died at a young 22 years old. Death certificate says he died of unknown cause at Memphis General Hospital.

McKenzie B. (1901)

McKenzie B. (1901)

Daisey C. (1903)

Dorothy (1903)

Isabel H. 1880-

DEATH RECORD

Name: Robert M Proctor
Birth Date: abt 1848
Birth Place: North Carolina
Age: 74
Death Date: 9 Nov 1922
Death Place: Memphis, Shelby, Tennessee
Burial Date: 9 Nov 1922
Burial Place: Memphis, Shelby, Tennessee
Cemetery Name: Popler Grove
Gender: Male
Race: White
Marital Status: Married
Residence Place: Memphis, Shelby, Tennessee
Occupation: Farmer
Mother's name: Kate Freidle
Mother's Birth Place: Tennessee

ROBERT'S DEATH CERTIFICATE

STATE OF TENNESSEE

GENERATION FOUR

Anderson Proctor (1815) and Elizabeth Vaughn (1828 -

Anderson was born and died in North Carolina - Orange
County.

Elizabeth was born in North Carolina, married Anderson in 1848
in Orange Co, NC and in 1900 was living in Salem, Forsyth Co,
NC with her son Solomon and his family.

Their children:

Jennifer Frances (1861-1946) married Edmund Dixon Woody and lived in Durham, NC

Robert

Solomon Doss 1856 –1935 / married Sarah Elizabeth Vernon / buried in NC.

GENERATION FIVE

Joseph Proctor (1806-1860) and Susan Willis (1815-)

Joseph was born and died in Orange County, NC.

Children:

Anderson 1815-

GENERATION SIX

Richard Anthony Proctor III (1780-1864) and Nancy Sallie Dollar (1785-1850)

Richard was born in Warren Co, NC and died in Orange County, NC. Nancy was also born and died in Orange County, NC. In the 1790 census he lived in Pitt Co, NC.

14 March 1791; May Ct. 1791. Acct. sale Est. BECKHAM (BUCKHAM) RAIMEY, dec'd. by JOHN MAYFIELD & WILLIAM ELLIS, Extrs. Purchasers:

14 March 1791- RICHARD PROCTOR was one of the purchasers at the estate sale of Beckham Raimey, dec'd. of Warren Co., NC.

Submitted by John Mayfield nad William Ellis, executors, to the Warren County May Court 1791. (Warren County, NC Will Book 6, pg. 1)

Thier children:

Nancy Proctor (1816-1890) married Davis Chisenhall

John S. (1819-after 1854) / married Mary Cook and had eight children.

William B. Proctor (1821-) married Susan G. ? in 1843 NC

Kinchen Proctor (1823-) married Nancy Oliver in 1842. also married Minerva Oliver in 1856.

Francis Marion Proctor Sr. (1830-1895) lived and died in Durham, NC. A civil war vet, a Sargeant in Company A, Mallett's Battalion, NC Camp Guards (Camp Holmes). He married Mildred Jane Pendergrass Proctor and had nine children.

Joseph 1806-1860)

Sterling (1803-after 1870) Orange County, NC/ married Winnie Green and had 15 children.

Oswell Kinion Proctor Sr. 1827-1863 - born in Orange Co, NC / died in Goldsboro, Wayne County, NC. . married . He died of disease. He was a private in 1863 in the vivil war into "G" company NC 3rd light artillery. Married Sarah Jane Barbee in 1848.

GENERATION SEVEN

Richard Proctor (1760-) and Lucretia Mabry Proctor (1762-1840)

Both born in Warren Co, NC and died in Orange Co.

Their children:

Richard Anthony (1780-1864) Orange Co, NC

Joseph (1784-1860) Orange Co., NC

John (1787-1816) Orange Co, NC

GENERATION EIGHT

Richard Proctor Jr. (1730 NC to) and Sarah

This Richard was born in North Carolina and in the 1790 census lived in Halifax, NC.

COURT RECORDS ON RICHARD PROCTOR Jr.

DB-2, page 31. 5 October 1767. RICHARD PROCTOR,JR. to WILLIAM EDWARDS, both of Bute Co. 12 Pds:l0Sh: Va. money for 100 A. in Bute Co. on ES Six Pound Creek adj. BENJAMIN EGERTON & JAMES EGEERON. Wit: WILLIAM HILL, EPHRAIM HILL. Ack: by RICHARD PROCTOR, Bute February Court 1768, BEN McCULLOCH, C.C. Reg: 4 May 1768, by WILLIAM JOHNSON, P.R. Marginal notation: 28th June Del to BEN EGERTON per your Ord.

February 1769. RICHARD PROCTOR & SARAH, his wife, to NATHANIEL BAXTER, carpinter, all of Bute Co. 25 Pds. Va. money (or Procl. money at 25%) for 240 a. in Bute Co. on BS Six Pound Creek adj. sd. PROCTOR, EDWARDS, BENJAMIN EGERTON & THOMAS PERSON. Wit: DANIEL PEGRAM, JR., WILLIAM BALTHROP, THOMAS EATON. Proven by WILLIAM BOLTHROP, Bute February Court, 1769, Ben McCULLOCH, C.C. Reg: 30 July 1769, by WILLIAM JOHNSON, P.R

JAMES NICHOLSON, JR., to BENJAMIN NICHOLSON. Dated 25 July 1764. 88 Pds. Va. money. Sale of all household goods, debts I now owe, livestock (including one cow of EDWARD HOLLOMAN'S mark & one sow with mark of LATER), my part of crops now in care of MOSES BEO(?). Red: Aug. Court 1764. Wit: THOS. MARTON, RICHARD PROCTOR, SAM'L NICHOLSON (BUTE COUNTY RECORD BOOK NO. 1) Richard Proctor, Jun'r William Edwards 100 A 10/05/1767 (Bute Co., North Carolina Court Minutes)

Ack: by RICHARD PROCTOR, Bute February Court 1768, BEN McCULLOCH, C.C. Reg: 4 May 1768, by WILLIAM JOHNSON, P.R. Marginal notation: 28th June Del to BEN EGERTON per your Ord. (Warren Co., North Carolina - Deeds)

3-6-1769--------------Richard Proctor (BUTE) 400 A. $FO: George Sugg (Pat. 1756)

April 1773. NATHANIEL BAXTER & PEGGY, his wife, to WOOD MALONE,all of Bute Co. 260 Pds. Va. money, or Procl. money at 33 1/3 %, for 300 A. in Bute Co. on BS Sixpound Creek, adj. PAINE, EDWARDS, BENJAMIN EGERTON, THOMAS PERSON & sd. BAXTER - and another 200 A. tract adj. sd. Baxter's Old Line,

PAINE & WORRELL, an EARL GRANVILLE grant to RICHARD PROCTOR. Wit. THOS. MILLER,SR., THOS. MILLER, JR., JAMES PAINE. Ack. by NATHANIEL BAXTER & PEGGY, his wife, shefirst consenting in private examination, Bute May Court , BEN McCULLOCH, C.C. Reg. 30 January 1775, by JAS. JOHNSON, P.R. (Deed Book 4, Warren County, NC)

August 1768. WILLIAM SHELL, of Brunswick Co., Va., to STEPHEN SHELL, of Bute Co. 100 Pds. Va. money for 250 A. in Bute Co., partof a grant to ARTHUR ATKINS, on Upper Run of Pegeon Roost Creek to Midle Runof sd. Creek, adj. ROBERSON, KING & BRITT(BRETT).Wit: JAMES MILLES, RICHD. PROCTOR,JR., STEPEN HANGRAVE,JR.Ack: by WILLIAM SHELL, Bute August Court 1768, BEN McCULLOCH, C.C.Reg: 15 January 1769, by WILLIAM JOHNSON, P.R.Marginal notation: Deld. 26th. July 1771 to MARMADUKE JOHNSON.

GENERATION NINE

Richard Proctor Sr. (1685 in Surry, Virginia) and Sarah

COURT RECORDS RELATED TO RICHARD Sr.

DB-2, page 31. 5 October 1767. RICHARD PROCTOR,JR. to WILLIAM EDWARDS, both of Bute Co. 12 Pds:l0Sh: Va. money for 100 A. in Bute Co. on ES Six Pound Creek adj. BENJAMIN EGERTON & JAMES EGEERON. Wit: WILLIAM HILL, EPHRAIM HILL. Ack: by RICHARD PROCTOR, Bute February Court 1768, BEN McCULLOCH, C.C. Reg: 4 May 1768, by WILLIAM JOHNSON, P.R. Marginal notation: 28th June Del to BEN EGERTON per your Ord.

February 1769. RICHARD PROCTOR & SARAH, his wife, to NATHANIEL BAXTER, carpinter, all of Bute Co. 25 Pds. Va. money (or Procl. money at 25%) for 240 a. in Bute Co. on BS Six Pound Creek adj. sd. PROCTOR, EDWARDS, BENJAMIN EGERTON & THOMAS PERSON. Wit: DANIEL PEGRAM, JR., WILLIAM BALTHROP, THOMAS EATON. Proven by WILLIAM BOLTHROP, Bute February Court, 1769, Ben McCULLOCH, C.C. Reg: 30 July 1769, by WILLIAM JOHNSON, P.R

JAMES NICHOLSON, JR., to BENJAMIN NICHOLSON. Dated 25 July 1764. 88 Pds. Va. money. Sale of all household goods, debts I now owe, livestock (including one cow of EDWARD HOLLOMAN'S mark & one sow with mark of LATER), my part of crops now in care of MOSES BEO(?). Red: Aug. Court 1764. Wit: THOS. MARTON, RICHARD PROCTOR, SAM'L NICHOLSON (BUTE COUNTY RECORD BOOK NO. 1) Richard Proctor, Jun'r William Edwards 100 A 10/05/1767 (Bute Co., North Carolina Court Minutes)

Ack: by RICHARD PROCTOR, Bute February Court 1768, BEN McCULLOCH, C.C. Reg: 4 May 1768, by WILLIAM JOHNSON, P.R. Marginal notation: 28th June Del to BEN EGERTON per your Ord. (Warren Co., North Carolina - Deeds)

3-6-1769--------------Richard Proctor (BUTE) 400 A. $FO: George Sugg (Pat. 1756)

April 1773. NATHANIEL BAXTER & PEGGY, his wife, to WOOD MALONE,all of Bute Co. 260 Pds. Va. money, or Procl. money at 33 1/3 %, for 300 A. in Bute Co. on BS Sixpound Creek, adj. PAINE, EDWARDS, BENJAMIN EGERTON, THOMAS PERSON & sd. BAXTER - and another 200 A. tract adj. sd. Baxter's Old Line,

PAINE & WORRELL, an EARL GRANVILLE grant to RICHARD PROCTOR. Wit. THOS. MILLER,SR., THOS. MILLER, JR., JAMES PAINE. Ack. by NATHANIEL BAXTER & PEGGY, his wife, shefirst consenting in private examination, Bute May Court , BEN McCULLOCH, C.C. Reg. 30 January 1775, by JAS. JOHNSON, P.R. (Deed Book 4, Warren County, NC)

August 1768. WILLIAM SHELL, of Brunswick Co., Va., to STEPHEN SHELL, of Bute Co. 100 Pds. Va. money for 250 A. in Bute Co., partof a grant to ARTHUR ATKINS, on Upper Run of Pegeon Roost Creek to Midle Runof sd. Creek, adj. ROBERSON, KING & BRITT(BRETT).Wit: JAMES MILLES, RICHD. PROCTOR,JR., STEPEN HANGRAVE,JR.Ack: by WILLIAM SHELL, Bute August Court 1768, BEN McCULLOCH, C.C.Reg: 15 January 1769, by WILLIAM JOHNSON, P.R.Marginal notation: Deld. 26th. July 1771 to MARMADUKE JOHNSON.

GENERATION TEN

Joshua Proctor (1650-1716) and Katherine Owens Proctor (1666-1717)

Joshua was born in Southwark Parrish, Surry, Virginia and died in VA.

Katherine Owens was also born in Southwark Parrish, Surry, VA. They married in 1681.

Katherine's parents are Bartholomew Owen (immigrant) and Joanna "Jane" Owens

Thier Children:

Richard Proctor Jr. 1730-

John

Nicholas

william

Elizabeth

COURT RECORDS FOR RICHARD PROCTOR JR.

Surry County Deed Book

In 1695 Robert Owen, the son, sold 110 acres of the same patent to Joshua Proctor [DB 5, p89] describing it as adjacent to Richard Jordan. This means Proctor's land bordered the Jordan plantation to the east, on the north bank of the Johnchecohuk Swamp. Joshua Proctor left this land in his 1718 will to his son Nicholas Proctor. When Nicholas Proctor sold the land, on 16 April 1746, he described it as land on Johnchecohunk Swamp adjacent Robert Jordan [DB 1741-6, p415].

Surry Co. Order Book, 1690-1718, p 105. and Ref Proctor: Surry Co., Va. Wills, Book 7, p. 207: PROCTOR, JOSHUA: Leg. To sons, Robert and Richard Proctor 566 acres of Land adjoining to Spring Branch... Mr. Richard Washington, and Henry Watkins on west side of son, Richard's house. To son Nicholas Proctor, 160 acres, where I how live. To daughter, ELIZABETH ROWLAND, 10 sheep. To daughter, Katherine, 40 shillings. To daughter Sarah, five pounds. Daughters, Mary and Hannah. Make son, Robert Exer. Wit: Nich. Smith, Allen Warren, Wm. Warren, Thomas Smith. Made 22 March 1717/18. Probated: 20 Jan.. 1719, Book 7, p. 235."

Surry County Will, Deeds, Book 4, " p. 178 6 Jan. 1690, JOSHUA PROCTER and wife, KATHERINE PROCTOR, of Southwarke Parish to Edward Newby, late of Lawnes Creek Parish... 450 acres between Johnchekockon Swamp (sp.?) and at the main Blackwater in Southwarke Parish. Land is 1/2 of the patent of 900 acres granted to William Rogers and myself on 20 April 1685. Land adjoins Robert Warren and Robert Owen. Signed Joshua (X) Proctor and Katherine (X) Proctor, Wit: Thomas Smith and Richard Jordan, Sr. Rec. 6 Jan. 1690."

Surry Co. Tithables of 1681 showed WILLIAM ROGERS & Joshua Procter husband of Katherine Owen (daughter of Jane and Bartholomew Owen):(18) For 1682 WILLIAM ROGERS only: For 1683 WILLIAM ROGERS 8. Rob Owen. In 1685 WILLIAM ROGERS & Joshua Proctor were granted 900 acres in Surry Co. For transporting 18 persons. (19) In 1686, after Jane's death, WILLIAM ROGERS I married second, ELIZABETH CARTWRIGHT, who was named in 1676 in the will of her father ROBERT CARTWRIGHT I of Surry Co. Va.

Their children:

Nicholas 1674-1775

Richard Proctor Sr. 1685-

Robert 1686-1754

Elizabeth 1689-1752 married William Rowland IV

George

Rowland 1691

Catherine 1694-1784 married Edward Grantham Jr.

> NOTE ABOUT CATHERINE: Per "The Heritage of Wayne
> County" about 1748, Edward and Catherine Grantham,
> Thomas and his five, Mary, John and his wife Ann cmae
> to what is now know as Grantham township, which at
> that time was in Johnson County, from Surry County,
> Virginia. Edward petitioned for Warrants for land in
> 1749. Fact #1. 1717. exchanged parcels of land with
> John Avery Fact #2. 1723, bought 460 acres bound by
> Coppohund Swamp and Blackwater Swamp for 20
> pounds.

Sarah 1694-

Mary 1696

Hannah 1698

Grey Thomas 1692

THE WILL OF JOSHUA

Wills: PROCTER, Joshua, 1718: Surry County, VA Probate 1/1719
Bk

Surry Co., VA, Deeds, Wills, Etc. 7 (1715-1730), pp. 235-36

In the Name of God Amen I Joshua PROCTER of Southwark psh:
being in perfect health, Sence, and Memory thanks be to
Almighty God for it: but Considering the uncertainty and frailty
of mans life do make ordain and appoint this to be my Last Will
and Testament Revoaking and Disannuling and Void all former
Wills made by me and this in manner and form as followeth

First and above all I bequeath my Soul into the hands of Almighty God that gave it me trusting in the Merritts of my Blessed Saviour Jesus Christ for a full and free pardon of all my willfull and frail Sins Committed in this wicked and Vicious Life. And my body to be buried in a Christian form at the discretion of my well beloved and dutyfull Chrildren [sic] and for what worldly Goods and Estate God of his Mercy has bestowed on me after all my Just Debts paid I Give and bequeath as following

I Give unto my Sons Robert and Richard PROCTER five hundred Sixty Six Acres of Land Joyning upon Mr Richard WASHINGTON and Henry WATKINS the dividing Line is upon upon a branch on the West side of my Son Richd house runing N.W. to a branch called a Spring branch from thence N.W. to a white wood tree standing in my Line I give it to them and their heirs for Ever~

I give unto my son Nicholas PROCTER One hundred and Sixty Acres of Land whereon I now live with all houses and Orchards and all advantages thereto belonging to him and his heirs for Ever~

I give unto my son Nicholas PROCTER one feather bed with the furniture belonging to it~

I give unto my son Richard PROCTER ten Shillings Curr:t mony

I give unto my Daughter Elizabeth ROWLAND ten Shillgs: Curr:t mony

I give unto my Daughter Katherine forty Shillings Current mony

I give unto my Daughter Sarah five pounds Currant mony

I Appoint my Loving Son Robert PROCTER my hole and Sole Executor of this my Will and Testament and I commit it to his

Charge and Care my two Daughters Mary & Hannah till they shall Come to the full age of one and twenty or Married and I give my said daughters upon the full age of one and twenty or Married five pounds a piece to be paid them either upon day of marryage or the full age of one and twenty which shall first happen by my Execut:r Robert PROCTER out of my moveable Estate which he the said Robert PROCTER can best Spare to them till he hath paid them both their five pounds a peice

In Witness hereof I have set my hand and Seal this 22:d day of March 1717/8

Joshuah PROCTOR: Sealed with red wax

Signed Sealed & Acknowledged to behis Will & desire in ye presents of

At a Court held for at Southwark for the County of Surry Jan:ry ye 20:th 1719 [1719/20]

The above menc'oned Will of Joshuah PROCTER deced: thus presented by Rob:t PROCTER Ex:r thereof who made Oath thereto and being proved by the Oaths of Allen WARREN Will: WARREN & Thomas SMITH Witnesses thereto the same was ordered to be

recorded and is recorded by~Jn:o ALLEN Cl Cur:a

SURREY COUNTY VA DEED BOOK - LAND OF JOSHUA AND FAMILY

Surry County Deed Book:

In 1695 Robert Owen, the son, sold 110 acres of the same patent to Joshua Proctor [DB 5, p89] describing it as adjacent to Richard Jordan. This means Proctor's land bordered the Jordan plantation to the east, on the north bank of the Johnchecohuk Swamp. Joshua Proctor left this land in his 1718 will to his son Nicholas Proctor. When Nicholas Proctor sold the land, on 16 April 1746, he described it as land on Johnchecohunk Swamp adjacent Robert Jordan [DB 1741-6, p415].

Surry Co. Order Book, 1690-1718, p 105. and Ref Proctor: Surry Co., Va. Wills, Book 7, p. 207: PROCTOR, JOSHUA: Leg. To sons, Robert and Richard Proctor 566 acres of Land adjoining to Spring Branch... Mr. Richard Washington, and Henry Watkins on west side of son, Richard's house. To son Nicholas Proctor, 160 acres, where I how live. To daughter, ELIZABETH ROWLAND, 10 sheep. To daughter, Katherine, 40 shillings. To daughter Sarah, five pounds. Daughters, Mary and Hannah. Make son, Robert Exer. Wit: Nich. Smith, Allen Warren, Wm. Warren, Thomas Smith. Made 22 March 1717/18. Probated: 20 Jan.. 1719, Book 7, p. 235."

Surry County Will, Deeds, Book 4, " p. 178 6 Jan. 1690, JOSHUA PROCTER and wife, KATHERINE PROCTOR, of Southwarke Parish to Edward Newby, late of Lawnes Creek Parish... 450 acres between Johnchekockon Swamp (sp.?) and at the main Blackwater in Southwarke Parish. Land is 1/2 of the patent of 900 acres granted to William Rogers and myself on 20 April 1685. Land adjoins Robert Warren and Robert Owen. Signed Joshua (X) Proctor and Katherine (X) Proctor, Wit: Thomas Smith and Richard Jordan, Sr. Rec. 6 Jan. 1690."

Surry Co. Tithables of 1681 showed WILLIAM ROGERS & Joshua Procter husband of Katherine Owen (daughter of Jane and

Bartholomew Owen):(18) For 1682 WILLIAM ROGERS only: For 1683 WILLIAM ROGERS 8. Rob Owen. In 1685 WILLIAM ROGERS & Joshua Proctor were granted 900 acres in Surry Co. For transporting 18 persons. (19) In 1686, after Jane's death, WILLIAM ROGERS I married second, ELIZABETH CARTWRIGHT, who was named in 1676 in the will of her father ROBERT CARTWRIGHT I of Surry Co. Va.

GENERATION ELEVEN

George Proctor (1621-1682) and wife   Elizabeth Ann Marriott Bishop (1621-1664)

Sept. 4, 1672 Cout proceedings show that the wife of George Proctor was formerly the wife of Major William Marriott, and before that the wife of John Bishop. Francis Mason was guardian of John Bishop, orphan.   I found one resource showing Elizabeth's maiden name as Norton.

George was born in Paces Paines, Jamestown, James City, Virginia and died in Southwark Parrish, Surry, VA.

George was an important figure in Bacon's Rebellion.

Their children:

George Jr. (1647-1730) Surry, VA to St. George Parish, Spotsylvania, VA

Joshua (1650-1716)

Mary (1652-

William (1665-1753)

JOHN HAD A SECOND WIFE ELIZABETH BURGESS MARRIOTT (1621-1672) .

BACON'S REBELLION FROM WIKIPEDIA

Bacon's Rebellion was an armed rebellion in 1676 by Virginia settlers led by Nathaniel Bacon against the rule of Governor William Berkeley. The colony's disorganized frontier political structure, combined with accumulating grievances (including leaving Bacon out of his inner circle, refusing to allow Bacon to be a part of his fur trade with the Native Americans, and Doeg tribe Indian attacks), helped to motivate a popular uprising against Berkeley, who had failed to address the demands of the colonists regarding their safety.

About a thousand Virginians of all classes rose up in arms against Berkeley, attacking Native Americans, chasing Berkeley from Jamestown, Virginia, and ultimately torching the capital. The rebellion was first suppressed by a few armed merchant ships from London whose captains sided with Berkeley and the loyalists.[2] Government forces from England arrived soon after and spent several years defeating pockets of resistance and reforming the colonial governnmnt to one more directly under royal control.[3]

It was the first rebellion in the American colonies in which discontented frontiersmen took part; a similar uprising in Maryland took place later that year. The alliance between former indentured servants and Africans against bond-servitude disturbed the ruling class, who responded by hardening the racial caste of slavery.[4][5][6] While the farmers did not succeed in their initial goal of driving Native Americans from Virginia, the rebellion did result in Berkeley being recalled to England.

Here's an engraving sketch from the 1800's about the Burning of Jamestown.

Of the above 40 men, it is again noteworthy that practically all were from Southwark Parrish . . . Most of the above men were small land-owners, several were freemen who worked on plantations belonging to others . . . George Proctor later became a Justice of the county, and had married the widow of Major William Marriott, a former Burgess. . .

Colonial Surry by John B. Boddie ~ Surry Couty in Bacon's Rebellion pps. 136-7

Will and Order Book

July 2, 1672. Petition of George Proctor, who married the relict of Major William Marriott.

Sept. 4, 1672 Cout proceedings show that the wife of George Proctor was formerly the wife of Major William Marriott, and before that the wife of John Bishop. Francis Mason was guardian of John Bishop, oe\\rphan.

DISTURBING STORY ABOUT GEORGE AND THE ABUSE OF HIS WIFE ELIZABETH

Court Case Against George Proctor in 1675 May 1675

From Surry Co., VA Records, FHC Film #0034099 (p78 & 79)

4 May 1675 - Thomas High gave a deposition in which he states he is 28 years old or thereabouts. "Examined and Sworn Saith:

That being at the house of Mr. Geo:Proctor ye first March last enquiring for Lt. Pittman and going in to light my pipe Mrs. Proctor told me he was at Mr. Summers, as ye deponent was going downe, Mrs. Proctor said she would go with me, and did soe, and when I came there as I was - discoursing with the said Pittman, Mr. Proctor as he was there sitting by the fire side asked his wife if she would goe home, who answered yes if he pleased, and when they were gone the Company that was theire went to the said Mr. Proctors, as also ye depont. and Lt. Pittman discoursing - about our business and the rest of the Company going in before us, ye depont. and said Pittman stayed at the gate some short time, and hearing of a great noyse within ye depont. asked Lt. Pittman whate was the matter, who answered he could not tell, and as we were therein talking the said Pittman asked ye depont. if he would not give him halfe a pinte who told him noe, then the said Pittman said I will Joyne with you, ye depont. answered he did not care if the did Joyne with him, we the

Depont. and the said Pittman, went into the said Mr. Proctors house and when we did and Proctor was calling his wife - Damd wh(---), and bitching wh(---) and Such Kind of languige, and then ye depot. asked the said Proctor if he would lett him have a half pint of drink he said he would pay him for it, but the said Proctor said Noe, but he would give me halfe a pinte, ye depont. answered he did not desire any upon - guift, but Lt. Pittman said he would accept it if he pleased, where upon the said Mr. Proctor called for somebody to draw it, and his wife rose up to give the fellow the keys which came to draw the drink, but Mr. Proctor called her back by the name of wh(---), and said she should not Stir, whereupon She went and satt downe againe in a chair by the fire, but the fellow went and brought half a pinte, and when it was out ye depont. asked if he would lett him have halfe a pinte, he replyed yes, it was also brought and ye depont. paid mony for, during the time his drink was drinking the said Proctor was abusing his wife by calling her wh(---) and Severall other bad languige - given to her, and ye depont. asked the said Proctor and desired him to be quiet and not use such terrible words which he Still continued doing, where upon ye depont. asked the said Proctor whose wh(---) she was, who replied she was ye deponts. for aught he knew, and Several others, but not naming anybody, ye depont. replyed he had Knowne her twenty years yet ye never know anyone give her Such a report, the said Procter replied she might be a wh(---) for all _____, ye depont. answered he could not tell wheather she was or noe, soe the said Proctor - went from his Company into his Chamber pretending he would goe to sleep, leaving his Wife Sitting by the fire in a chair. The Company at the table talking and laughing, ye said Proctor came out againe from the room and calling his Wife wh(---) and bitch and such kind of terms, and Saying thee was among her Rouges, ye nor any of the Company not giving him one word, then he went into his rooms againe, after he was gone Some of the Company drank to her, who took the cup and drank to Some of the Company, and immediately the said Proctor came running out calling her wh(---), and saying now she was with her delight, with that he pulled her and halted her and pushed her and Swore he would make her doe as he would have her do. She answered anything that he would have her doe, she would doe provided he would be quiett, he replied he would make her, she asked him whet he would have her doe, wheather she should come and Sitt by him or wheather he would goe to sleepe, he replyed he would goe to sleepe soe they both went into the other room, and she Sat by him he pretending he would go to sleepe, but immediately as we Sat at the table, we heard her Cry out Murder, thereupon the Company said one to another doe you goe in, but none of these did, whereupon ye depont. went in, and asked Proctor what was the Matter, he said not was that to me, ye depont. asked him, if he were minded to doe any Murder, he said what was it to me, I told him theire Should be noe Murder done as long as ye depont. was in the house if he could help it, during this discourse Capt. Swann came in, and ye depont. asked Capt Swann to go into the roome to him, whereupon Capt. Swann went in asked what was the matter, but what answer the said Proctor made ye depont. know not, Soe Capt. Swann and the said Proctor went toward Mr. Summers, leaving Mrs. Proctor Crying upon the bed, and further ye depont. saith not.

Signed Tho (mark) High

Sworn before Col. Tho:Swann

Lt. Col. Geo:Jordan and Maj. Wm 1675

Browne 4 May 1675 _____William Edwards, Clerk

May 5 1675

W. E. Clk"

Tho:Pittman, Sr, age 60 or thereabouts, also gave a deposition in which he stated..."being at the house of Mr. Geo. Proctor upon the 1st day of March about 8 o'clock in the morning...Mr Proctor was drinking of burnt sack* and did finde that Mr. Proctor had drank to much...he also stated that Mr. Proctor and his wife were good friends but within two or three hours of drinking he ralled at his wife...Mr. Thompson and Tho:High did _____ her away, after she put on her coat...and I left and went away, but before I went Mr. Geo. Proctor went and fetched his Sword, then told his wife..." (p76)

Isabell Forbus, age 50 years or thereabouts, gave a deposition also in which she said she had "met Col. Swann and Mr. Proctor as she was walking and that...Mr Proctor asked her to speak to his wife and she said she would. She arrived at their home and shortly after Mr. Proctor came in then "went into another roome and fetched his Sword removing toward his wife ye depont went and stood between them...one Tho:High came in an delivered Mr Proctor to be ruled by his friends and be quiett, and Mr Proctor answered he had to many such friends as he was..." The depositions above seem to be after Geo. Proctor had gone with Capt. Swann and then come back to his home (FHC film # 0034099, p76)

Capt. Robt Spensor and Benja Thompson also made statements. (Same film # as above, p74/5)

6 Mar 1682 - Thomas High is listed as owing the Estate of Geo. Proctor (FHC Film #0034099, Surry Co. Records, 1671-1684)

GENERATION TWELVE

Planter John Proctor (1583-1627) and Alice Graye (1587-1627)

John was born in Middlesex England and died in 1627 in Paces Paines, Jamestown, VA. He was 44 years old.

Alice was born in London, England and died in Jamestown, VA. She was 41.

John came to America in 1610 on the ship DELIVERANCE. He made a second trip with supplies on the ship SEAVENTURE His story is below. After leaving Jamestown, VA they migrated to Surrey, VA. John Proctor received a patent for land from the Virginia Company in July of 1623. and received 100 acres in Henrico on the James River in 1626. John died in 1624 and his will mentions his brother Thomas, a haberdasher in London.

ALICE - was a hero and saved the family land from Indian attacks during the time in Jamestown.

Their children:

Robert (1617-1695) married Rachel Beard Stimpson. He went to Maryland 1660.

> Rachel Beard is related to the following famous people :
>
> Ancestry.com has a list of 13 Famous People related to Rachel Beard. Here are some of these: Charles Carroll of Carrollton(1737-1832), Maryland Representative, 1st Cousin 3 times removed; William Randolph Hearst(1863-1951), Newspaper magnate, Relationship: 6th Great Grandson through her daughter, Elizabeth Clarke; Rutherford Birchard Hayes(1822-1893), 19th President of the United States of America, 3rd Cousin 5 times removed; John Ledyard(1751-1789), American Explorer; 4th Cousin 3 times removed; Howard Hughes(1905-1976), American Aviator, 2nd Cousin 8 times removed; William Howard Taft(1857-1930), 27th President of the United States of America, 3rd Cousin 6 times removed, etc.

George (1621-1682)

William (1622-

John (1622-

Richard (1623-

Brother Thomas

FIND A GRAVE BIOGRAPHY

John Graye Proctor was born in 1583 in London, London, England. He was the son of John Nicholas Proctor (1557-1600) and Alles Graye Proctor (1561-1600).

John made his first trip to Virginia in 1607 at the age of 24. This voyage made the history books. The "Sea Venture" (also called the Seaventure or Sea Adventure) sailed as part of a flotilla of nine ships commanded by Admiral Sir George Somers. Intended destination was Jamestown, Virginia. The On 2 June 1609, "Sea Venture", flagship of the "Third Supply" (six ships and two pinnances); departed London. On 23 July, A hurricane at sea separated the Sea Venture from the other vessels. After four days, she began taking on water. Land was sited and she wrecked between two reefs off the shores of Bermuda on 28 July 1609. All of approximately 150 passengers safely made land. Two pinnances were built during the following nine months, the "Deliverance" and the "Patience". These vessels sailed on to Virginia 10 May 1610. One of the passengers on this trip was John Rolfe, a young man in his twenties and traveling with his wife. Their baby girl was born in Bermuda, christened Bermudas and died shortly thereafter. His wife died shortly after reaching Virginia Spring 1610 and he married Pocahontas in April 1614.

John married Alice "Allis" Graye (1587-1627) in London, England in 1610. Allis was the daughter of William Graye (1564-1607) and Elizabeth Larye Graye (1561-1600).

John Graye and Alice Graye Proctor were the parents of the following known

Their children:

William Proctor,

John Proctor,

Robert Proctor,

Daughter Proctor,

George Proctor

 Richard Proctor.

GREAT STORY ABOUT JOHN AND ALICE

Even though the 1625 muster states that John Proctor, an ancient planter, reached Virginia in 1607 on the Seaventure, it is much more likely that he came to the colony in 1609-1610 in one of the vessels that comprised part of Sir Thomas Gate's fleet. In December 1617 Proctor was identified as a debtor in the will made by Robert Smalley of Bermuda Hundred39.

Sometime after 1621 he wed Alice (Allis, Allice), whom Captain John Smith described as a proper gentlewoman. By early 1622 the Proctor couple had established a plantation70 on the lower side of the James River within the corporation of Henrico.

According to Captain John Smith, on March 22, 1622, when the Indians attacked the sparsely scattered settlements along the banks of the James River, Mrs. Alice Proctor single-handedly defended the family home, which was adjacent to what became known as Proctor's Creek. In the wake of the Indian attack, the Proctors, like other colonists living near the head of the James River, were ordered to withdraw to positions of greater safety. As soon as the Proctors abandoned their home, the Indians returned and destroyed it. In 1623 John Proctor, who said he had been in Virginia for 14 years, was among those who refused Captain Nathaniel Butler's allegations about the colony. On June 25, 1623, the Virginia Company agreed to give John Proctor a patent for transporting 100 people to Virginia. he in turn, agreed to serve as an attorney for two London merchants so that he could recover funds they were owed by the late Hugh Crowder. Proctor also was supposed to send the two merchants' surplus goods to Virginia. On February 16, 1624, John and Alice Proctor and their servants were living at Paces Paines9 on land they were renting. They were still there February 4, 1625, and were well provisioned and outfitted with defensive weaponry. The Proctors apparently had become hardened to life, for in October 1624 they were brought before the authorities and accused of causing the death of a servant girl they had ordered flogged with stout cord and fishhooks. Court testimony provided by some of the Proctors' servants suggests that they were guilty and that they also were responsible for the death of another servant. Moreover, the Proctors were accused of detaining another planter's servant. In May 1625 John proctor was credited with 100 acres within the corporation of Henrico, the plantation he and his wife had seated prior to the 1622 Indian attack. By July 3, 1627, John proctor was dead, at which time his widow, Alice, presented the justices of the General Court with an inventory of his estate and was designated his administrator.

Among the debts Alice was authorized to collect on her husband's behalf were sumsowed by a Dutch carpenter and a man who had lost Proctor's small boat (SR 3112; SH 4; VCR 2:835, 457; 3:611; 4:425-246, 466-467, 552; CBE:40, 59; CJS 2:303; MCGC 12-13, 22-24, 54, 62, 78 150; DOR 1:38)

Virginia Immigrants and Adventurers, 1607-1635: A Biographical Dictionary By Martha W. McCartney. Genealogical Publishing Com, Apr 30, 2007 - Reference - 833 pages.

** It is disturbing that they flogged their servants with fishhooks and cord. If you see from the above story, they were responsible for several deaths of their servants.

** MENTIONED ABOVE IS THE EASTER ATTACK OF 1622 *

According to English accounts, Opechancanough planned to attack the Jamestown fort as well as the outlying settlements. But a young Indian boy who had been Christianized by the settlers forewarned the inhabitants. The news did not spread fast enough, however, to save the English living in the settlements.

On the day prior to the attack, the Indians came bringing gifts of meats and fruits and shared them with the settlers, thereby disguising their intentions. The following morning they circulated freely and socialized with the settlers before suddenly seizing their own work tools to attack them (See Robert Beverley's Description of the 1622 Attack). The Indians killed families in the plantation houses and them moved on to kill servants and workers in the fields. The Powhatans killed 347 settlers in all - men, women, and children. Not even George Thorpe, a prominent colonist well known for his friendly stance towards the Indians, was spared. The Powhatans harsh treatment of the bodies of their victims was symbolic of their contempt for their opponents. The Indians also burned most of the outlying plantations, destroying the livestock and crops.

The colonists in Jamestown were in an uproar, stunned by the massacre. The settlers immediately withdrew to the fort and to other easily defensible locations. In addition to the loss of life, the colonists also lost valuable crops and supplies necessary to survive the winter. Ironically, during the winter of 1622-23 the colonists were forced to trade with the Indians for corn and supplies and even with these provisions many went hungry. The mortality rate during the winter of 1622-23 climbed due to malnutrition and disease - over four hundred settlers died.

ALICE GRAYE

Alice Proctor, who lived on Proctor's creek near Richmond, and who, in 1622, defended her plantation against savages with great bravery. She is referred to as "Mistress Proctor, a proper, civill, modest gentlewoman." She afterwards refused to obey the order of the council to abandon her house for a safer location at Jamestown, and would not retire till the officers threatened to burn it down. She was widow of John Proctor.

There is a video on youtube about Mrs. Alice Proctor and the Indian attack at the colony of Jamestown, VA in 1622. Here is the link to this 2 minute video:

http://www.youtube.com/watch?v=nQoZ_5WxsGY&feature=youtu.be

Alice died aft 1627 in Pace's Paines, Jamestown, James City County, VA. She was 40 years old.

Pace's Paines was a 600 acre farm on the bluff across from the James River.

GENERATION THIRTEEN

John Nicholas Proctor (1559-) and Alice Proctor (1561-1600)

Both were born in London, Middlesex, England

Their children:

Planter John (1583-1627) Jamestown VA settler

Thomas 1587-1622) married Jane Squier Thomas Proctor Arrived Jamestown 1623 on the Ship SS Mary Providence

Anthony (1590)

Joshua (1600) Joshua Proctor whom Arrived Jamestown, VA. On Feb 1619 on the Ship SS Gift of God

Ambrose Proctor Sr. - born Isle of Wight, VA.   1600 Ambrose Proctor (1) the son of John Nicholas Proctor and Alice Gray had several brothers, John Proctor the Ancient Planter that Arrived at Jamestown, James City Co., VA 1611 on Salvage Barge of the SS SeaVenture and later moved to Surry Co., VA. after 1622. Joshua Proctor whom Arrived Jamestown, VA. On Feb 1619 on the Ship SS Gift of God. Thomas Proctor Arrived Jamestown

1623 on the Ship SS Mary Providence. Thomas Proctor was a wealthy London merchant. His will was dated 1634 in England and named his wife Jane and Son Samuel Proctor. His Will was published in the Virginia Magazine of History and Biography, Richmond Va., July 1904 Vol. 12, Issue 1. Anthony Proctor Arrived Upper Norfolk Co., VA., on the Ship SS Assurance. The lines of Ambrose, Joshua, and John Proctor survived and flourished in the New World. He arrived in Virginia in 1637

John (1595-1672) born in London, married Martha Harper and

JOHN (1595-1672) SON – JOHN – FIRST MALE TO BE ACCUSED OF WITCHRAFT IN SALEM

He married a Martha ?, Elizabeth Thorndike and Elizabeth Bassett. He sailed to New England in 1635. Died in Ipswich, Essex, Massachussetts.   John lived in Salem, Massachusetts and was part of the Salem Witch Trials. He was the first male accused of witchcraft, convicted and brought to prison. He was made to confess and sign a document.

John was a successful farmer, tavern keeper who lived on the edge of Salem, which is today Peabody, MA. He had considerable wealth and prestige. Proctor ran a tavern out of the same house in Peabody MA . (348 Lowell St.).

John Proctor, an early opponent of the witch hunt, lived in this house in 1692. One of the afflicted girls, Mary Warren, was a maidservant in his household. Proctor had cured her fits with a good whipping and maintained that the others could be cured with similar treatment. The stream which runs behind the house is known to this day as Proctor Brook. The Proctor house is privately owned.

Proctor seems to have been an enormous man, very large framed, "impulsive," with great force and energy. Proctor is described on several occasions, from various sources as a strong-willed beast of a man. Charles Upham writes, "He was a man of Herculean frame...he had great native force and energy...he was bold in his spirit and in his language." Although an upright man, he seems to have been rash in speech, judgment, and action. It was his unguarded tongue—that would eventually lead to his death.

John Proctor continued to challenge the veracity of spectral evidence and the validity of the Court of Oyer and Terminer which led to a petition signed by 32 neighbors in his favor. The signatories stated that Proctor had lived a 'Christian life in his family and was ever ready to help such as stood in need.'

John and Elizabeth Proctor were tried on August 5, 1692. They were both found guilty and sentenced to hang. Still maintaining his innocence, Proctor prepared his will but left his wife with nothing. Someassume that he did this as he assumed his wife would be executed as well. Proctor was executed on August 19, 1692, along with George Burroughs, John Willard, George Jacobs, Sr., Rebecca Nurse (Daughter of our ancestor)and Martha Corey.

The executed "witches" were thrown into shallow holes in the ledge under Gallows Hill. Some brave members of the Proctor family located John's body and removed it, secretly burying it on the grounds of their homestead (which they no longer legally owned). As for Elizabeth, since pregnant at the time of her condemnation, she was able to avoid execution at her appointed time, and gave birth to a child two weeks after John's execution. Thus, her unborn child saved her life. In May of 1693, Govenor Phips pardoned the remaining accused of witchcraft. Although pardoned, she was still a convicted felon in the eyes of the law and barred from claiming any of her husband's property as a result. On December 17, 1710, 578 pounds and 12 shillings was paid to her in restitution for her husband's death.

The Crucible by Arthur Miller, a fictionalized version of the trials casts John Proctor as one of the main characters in the play. Proctor is portrayed as being in his thirties and Abigail Williams is 17 and a half years old, while the real John Proctor and Abigail Williams were respectively about sixty and eleven years old at the time of the witch trials. In the play, they had an affair, as a result of which Abigail accused Elizabeth Proctor of witchcraft. In reality, Elizabeth Proctor was initially named by Ann Putnam on March 6, alleging that Proctor's spectre attacked the girl. She was accused by Abigail on March 14 and further accusations were made by Mercy Lewis. Miller has Mary Warren accuse Proctor of afflicting her but this followed his initial accusation by Abigail in early April 1692. There is no historical evidence to suggest that Abigail even knew John Proctor before she accused him of witchcraft.

In the 1996 film based on the play, Proctor was played by Daniel Day-Lewis.

GENERATION FOURTEEN

William Proctor (1506) and Isabel Lilburn or Lilborne (1506)

William was born 1506 in Nether Bordley, Yorkshire, England and died in Embleton Parish, Northumberland, England.

Isabel was born in Shawdon, Northumberland, England. Her parents are John Lilbourne .

William Proctor married Isabel Lilburn in December 1500. She was the daughter of John Lilburn of West Lilburn who also owned the manors of Shawdon, Glanton and Bedford, all of which were located in Northumberland. The Lilburns bought the manor around 1403.

The Proctor family, originally settled in Nether Bordley, Yorkshire, was established at Shawdon in 1506 through the marriage of William Proctor of Nether Bordley to Isabel, daughter of John Lilburn of Shawdon. John Proctor who exchanged Shawdon for the Dunstan estate, married twice. Thomas Proctor, the eldest son of the first marriage, became ultimately the owner of Rock, whilst John Proctor, the second son of the second marriage, succeeded under his fathers will to the land at Dunstan. The old tower, formerly known as Dunstan Hall, received from its new owners the name Proctor's Stead, by which it is generally known. But though the name of the Proctors remains associated with the place, the family did not retain the property for any great length of time. John Proctor, son of John Proctor and Elizabeth Ion, sold his land at Dunstan in 1778 to Daniel Craster for 7,700 pounds. In this way the old estate of the Wetwangs was added to that part of Dunstan which from ancient times had been the property of the Craster family. The boundries of Dunstan belonging to John Proctor were surveyed in 1724 and showed the "west farm" containing 359 acres, another farm containing 219 acres for a total of 578 acres.

Their children with Katherine:

Evan 1546-1647

Cuthbert   1558- married Margaret Roddam

John Nicholas 1559-1600 married _____- Graye. John's son Robert married Sarah FLETCHER

Thomas 1550-1624

Christopher 1560-1649

His other children with other wives:

Eustace

Barbara

Dosabell

Dorothy

GENERATION FIFTEEN

Geoffrey Proctor (1450-1525) and Margaret Bullock, 2nd wife is Katherine (1455-1525) and 3rd wife Alice West.   Margaret Bullock was born in Normande, France.

Geoffrey was born in Craven, Yorkshire, England and died in Nether Bordley, Yorkshire, England. He married Katherine in 1506.

His children with Katherine

Geoffrey

Richard P. (1480-1524)

Henry was a priest (-1524)

Robert   (1482-1524) born in London, died in Paces Paines, Jamestown

William 1480-1557- married Isabel Lilburn

Sir William 1482-1524

William Beauchamp-Proctor Sir   1506-1557

At the opening of the sixteenth century, the Procters were a vigorous race in Craven. At various houses in the township of Bordley, in the parish of Burnsall and at Winterburn, Friarshead and Cowpercote, in the parish of Gargrave, were established substantial families of the name, all tenants of Monastic Houses. It was a common practice of these establishments to lease the more remote portions of their landed property for terms of years at fixed rentals. By renewal of leases such properties were often held by successive generations of one family, a continuity of possession which conferred a measure of territorial importance.

Of such a family, Geoffrey Procter of Bordley, a tenant of the Abbey of Fountains, was the representative. He died in the second half of 1523 or early in the following year, and his long and very interesting will proves him to have possessed a very considerable estate both in lands and goods. In a deed of the twenty-sixth year of Henry VIII (Calton Deeds, 56), he is described as 'Geoffrey Procter auditor deceased', and from a petition to the monarch last mentioned ("Yorks. Record Series XIV, p152 - Star Chamber Proceedings), it appears that he was 'auditor' to Henry, Earl of Northumberland, a position which was perhaps analogous to that of the agent of to-day.

By his will dated 'at Nether Bordley in Craven the tend daye of Jany' in the sixteenth year of Henry VIII -1524 (Printed in Test. Ebor, V, 182. Surtees Soc. Vol 79), Geoffrey directs that in case he shall die within twenty miles of his parish church of Rilston, he shall be there buried with his wife. He proceeds to charge his lands in Litton, Owlcoottes, Hawkeswike and Scothorp in Craven,

PART OF GEOFFREY'S WILL

To his grandson Geoffrey Proctor, testator gives his 'signeth of gold that haith an hynde gravyn in the printe of it', and desires that he may 'be putto service to my singular good lorde my Lorde Percy at such tyme as it please his lordship to take hym to his service'. To his grandchildren Eustace and Henry he gives his 'best salte with a cover of silver parcell gilt XII silver spones, a goblet of silver with a cover parcell gilt and a litle macer withoute a cover, equally to be divided betwixt them'; to his son Richard 'six silver spoones and the goblett of silver with a cover and the salte of silver with a cover'; to his grandson Henry his 'best houp of gold' and one 'houp' of gold each to Eustace and Cuthbert Proctor, the latter's having a 'septer uppon it'.

Geoffrey devises his 'farmeholds' at Bordley to his eldest son Richard, and his lands in Malham, Kirkby, Calton and Hanlith to his grandson Geoffrey, son of his son Robert. He also makes provision for Eustace and Henry, sons of his son William. As supervisors of his will, he names 'Maister John Norton, of Norton, Esquier, Maister Antony Clifford, Esquier, Henry Marton, Richarde Banke, and John Lamberte, gentilmen'. The will was proved on 6 July 1525.

After the Dissolution, Bordley was included in a large slice of the lands of Fountains sold by Henry VIII to Sir Richard Gresham (Burton, Monast, p. 143). Ten years later in the fifth year of Edward VI, Sir Richard's son, John Gresham, sold the Bordley estate to John White, citizen and grocer of London for £474 10s 0d (Procter Deeds and Fine Trin. Term, 7 Edw. VI -1553) and in the eighteenth year of Elizabeth (1575-6), White, in turn, sold it for £780 to John Tennant, John Kidd and John Wallock. (Procter Deeds and Fine Trin. Term, 18 Eliz. -1576). Meantime, the Procters appear to have remained in possession of Bordley as tenants of its lay owners, but before the thirty ninth year of Elizabeth (1597) they had acquired the freehold, and it seems probable that the purchase last mentioned was made on their behalf.

In 1597, John Procter, who was possibly a younger son of Richard Procter of Bordley, was owner of the estate. He died on 24 November of that year, and Livery of his lands was granted to his son and heir, Thomas, in the forty-second year of the same reign (Pocter deeds). The grant shows that John held in chief by the service of the hundredth part of a knight's fee, the capital messuage called Bordley Hall, in Nether Bordley, ten messuages, ten gardens, ten orchards, one water corn-mill, two hundred acres of arable land, one hundred acres of meadow, two hundred acres of pasture, two hundred acres of moor, two hundred acres of turbary, and three hundred acres of gorse and heather, with all appurtenances of the said manor or capital messuage in Over Bordley, Nether Bordley, Kirkby, Burnsall and

Malham; also the advowson of the Vicarage of Gargrave and three messuages with ten bovates of land belonging to them in the same vill.

GENERATION SIXTEEN

Geoffrey (1430-1456) and Margaret Kirby (1425-1460)

GENERATION SEVENTEEN

Robert Proctor (1410-1440) and Mary Hawley (1410-

both born in England . Mary was born in Christ Church, Surrey, England

Their children:

Geoffrey 1430-1456

GENERATION EIGHTEEN

Robert Proctor 1390 -1430 and Joannet Hagthorpe (1385

born and died in England.

Their children:

Robert 1410-1440

3 boys, 1 girl

FURTHER LINES

Documentary research has traced the history of the township
back to Domesday Book, of course. In 1134 there is evidence of
the township belonging to Furness Abbey, before becoming part
of Fountains Abbey between 1149 and 1540. Specific references
to the granges of Nether and Over Bordley are mentioned as
early as 1198. With the Reformation, the township passed into
the hands of Sir Richard Gresham, John Whtye, and finally to
the Proctors, and their descendants, the Chadwick-Knowles
family, who still own land here.

Here's a picture of Shawdon Hall

THE ORIGINAL DUNSTANBURGH CASTLE

DUNSTAN CASTLE RENAMED PROCTOR'S STEAD

Another view of Proctors Stead - Dunstan estate

FOUNTAINS ABBEY FOUNDED 1132

But despite its financial problems, Fountains Abbey remained of considerable importance in the Cistercian Order. The abbots sat in Parliament and the abbacy of Marmaduke Huby (1495-1526) marked a period of revival. Fountains once again flourished, but its life was brought to an abrupt end in 1539 by Henry VIII's Dissolution of the Monasteries.

For a few months after the Dissolution, the abbey buildings stood empty in the hope of being the site for the cathedral for a new Dales bishopric. This was not to be, and by 1540 glass and lead from the dismantling of Fountains had found their way to Ripon and York.

Fountains Abbey was founded in 1132 where over 500 acres of land were sold by Henry VIII to Sir Richard Gresham, a merchant. The property was passed down through several generations of Sir Richard's family, finally being sold to Stephen Proctor who built Fountains Hall, an Elizabethan mansion built partly with stone from the abbey ruins, between 1598 and

1604. In 1767 it was sold for £18,000 to William Aislabie, who landscaped the abbey ruins to make a picturesque view from the Water Garden.

Fountain Abbey

Fountain abbey church

ENGLISH ESTATES OF THE PROCTOR FAMILY ESTATE: LANGLEY PARK:

On the River Yare, 10 miles South East of Norwich, England. This noble mansion is the home of Sir William Beauchamp Proctor, Bart., a vice admiral, in the Royal Navy. It was commenced in 1720 for Mr. Recorder Berney, who before it was completed, sold the property to George Proctor, Esquire, and he, dying in 1744, bequeathed it, with a considerable estate, to his nephew, William Beauchamp proctor, Esquire, who in memory of his Uncle, and with "Royal Permission," changed his name to Sir William Beauchamp Proctor, Bart., and Knight Champion of the Bath. By him, the mansion was much enlarged and beautified, and, upon his death in 1773, he was succeeded by his son, Sir Thomas Beauchamp Proctor, who then died in 1827. The estate then devolved to Sir William Proctor, the last named Baronet. Langley Hall or Langley Park is a magnificent structure, the center or main building is in five divisions with a portico of the Doric order, but the two original wings have been pulled down and rebuilt by Sir William Proctor, who has likewise added much to the comfort and convenience of the mansion. Few English county seats are richer than Langley Park in works of art, of the very finest order. We have only to name (Michael Angelo, Salvator Rosa, Nicholas Berghem, Canaletti, Vanervelde, Andre del Sarta, Wonverman, Teniers, Vandyke, Leonardo di Vinci, Claude, Albert Durer, and two Poussins, Murills, and Cornelins Jansen;) The Langley Park possesses an agreeable variety of surface, and is covered with extensive plantations and fine timber. One part in particular deserves notice being a walk from the east door to the church, through a shrubbery and pleasant ground that are kept in excellent order.

ESTATE: LONGLEY HALL, In Almondsbury, County of York, England: Owned by Ramsden Proctor in 1531.

ESTATE LANGLEY CASTLE, TOWN OF ALLENDALE, NORTHUMBERLAND, WSW OF Newcastle of Tyne on East Allen River (Photo in "Romance of Northumberland, page 254, U of R.)

ESTATE NETHER BORDLEY, WEST RIDING OF YORKSHIRE, East of Grassington, England, Owned by Geoffrey Proctor in 1456 and William Proctor in 1480.

www.ingramcontent.com/pod-product-compliance
Lightning Source LLC
Chambersburg PA
CBHW050751290526
45792CB00008B/2136